APPLIQUÉ PATTERNS
FROM
NATIVE
AMERICAN
BEADWORK
DESIGNS

DR. JOYCE MORI

American Quilter's Society
P. O. Box 3290 • Paducah, KY 42002-3290

All photographs by Richard Walker

Library of Congress Cataloging-in-Publication Data

Mori, Joyce
        Appliqué patterns from Native American beadwork designs / Joyce
Mori.
                p.   cm.
        Includes bibliographical references.
        ISBN 0-89145-826-3 : $14.95
            1. Appliqué--Patterns.   2. Indian beadwork.   I. Title.
    II. Title: Native American beadwork designs.
    TT779.M67 1993
    746.3--dc20   93--44235
                                                                        CIP

Additional copies of this book may be ordered from:

American Quilter's Society
P.O. Box 3290
Paducah, KY 42002-3290
@14.95. Add $1.00 for postage and handling.

✦ ACKNOWLEDGMENTS ✦

To all the unknown Native American and Metis artisans
who produced the beautiful beadwork pieces
from which I derived the inspiration for the designs in this book,
I owe a deep debt of gratitude.

To my husband John
who continually supports my work, offers helpful criticism,
and exhibits patience when the housework is not done,
I give my love and thanks.

To my mother who unfortunately is no longer alive
but who gave me my love of quilts and quilting,
I give heart felt thanks for this gift.

To God I give thanks for my life on this earth
allowing me to pursue work I truly love.

TABLE OF CONTENTS

⟬ INTRODUCTION ⟭

Plate 1.

Plate 2.

Most of the designs in this book are adapted from beaded objects made by members of Native American Indian tribes located in five major regions in North America. However, a few motifs were modified from Native American moosehair and silk embroidery decorative techniques. While the lovely floral motifs of the thread embroidery work cannot be overlooked, these last two technologies did not spread as rapidly as the idea of beadwork decoration; thus not as many examples of the artifacts remain to be studied.

American Indians desired glass beads as a trade item. In 1760, a six-foot string of beads could be purchased with a single beaver skin. But less than fifty years later, the same skin purchased two pounds of beads. Catholic priests also used the popular trade beads to help them in their religious conversion attempts. These missionaries gave away the beads to obtain the goodwill of the Indians and to reward Native American children for memorizing religious lessons. In addition to the beads, the Indians wanted the European cloth from which they sewed many clothing items. These pieces of apparel were then decorated with beads. Such fabric was a colorful substitute for animal hides.

For Native Americans, using beading extensively on clothing was not common until the nineteenth century. Prior to this time, the high cost and large size of the beads limited this artistic cultural expression. However, women in many tribes did produce items with designs made from dyed porcupine quills.

By 1775 Indians in the eastern United States obtained a tiny cut bead at British trading posts. An even smaller size bead, known as the seed bead, appeared about 1800. This has been the most common type of bead found in beadwork ever since. These finer glass beads were imported into the United States from several European countries and later from Japan. Once the Indians obtained large quantities of the smaller beads, the amount of beadwork done on their clothing and possessions expanded. These beads were easier to use, more colorful, and provided more opportunity for designing than had embroidery with porcupine quills.

Various tribal groups in several regions of North America developed floral beadwork and moosehair and silk embroidery work to high levels of artistic excellence. These beaded and embroidered objects have provided a beautiful legacy of designs that I have adapted into floral appliqué quilt designs. Figure 1 shows a map of these general regions. The first region includes the tribes of the Northeastern Woodland area, basically encompassing tribes in the northern half of the United States, west to the Mississippi River and north into the Canadian provinces of Quebec and Ontario. The early floral designs used in the beadwork by the tribes of the Great Lakes region were probably introduced by the Europeans, mostly the French. One notices a similarity between the flower shapes in the beadwork and Jacobean style crewel embroidery.

The second area includes tribes of the Great Plains region. This covers the states of North and South Dakota, Wyoming, and Montana and includes parts of the Canadian provinces of Manitoba, Saskatchewan, and Alberta. These tribes are more noted for their varied geometric patterns, but some floral designs were part of the mix. Indians from the Midwestern and Eastern area, who were employed by the fur trading companies, brought the idea of floral designs on beadwork into the Great Plains area, the Plateau, and later into the Yukon and Alaska. Men from these tribes were hired by fur trading companies to serve as guides. They moved into a region, married local Indian women, and showed them their designs. They wanted their wives to use these designs on clothing items. The women copied the ideas, but they changed the designs to reflect their environment and cultural traditions. Thus you see floral designs in these western regions, but through time they became different from those of the Northeastern Woodland tribes.

Beadwork in the Plains region was rarely done prior to 1840. But from 1890 to the 1920's the art form reached its

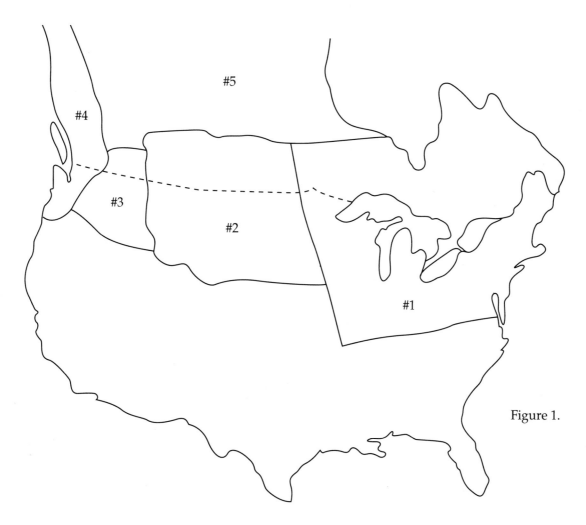

Figure 1.

high point. Practically everything made showed at least some beadwork, and ceremonial items were heavily beaded. This time frame reflected the period when the native culture was being destroyed, and the tribes were forced onto reservations. So beadwork appears to have been an expression of beauty in a world full of discouragement. Women had the time to practice and perfect this skill since they no longer were pursuing the arduous tasks of their native way of life. Pieces of beadwork were also sold for cash to visitors to the reservations.

Today the Plains Cree do more beadwork than other Plains groups because of the importance of the powwow among the Cree. Highly decorated costumes are desired by the dancers, so there is a market for beaded garments. There are also some handicraft cooperatives that provide an outlet for beadwork sales to the non-Indian market.

The third geographic region is the Plateau area where tribes such as the Flathead, Nez Perce, and other groups of the Columbia River region produced floral beadwork designs on beaded bags referred to as Plateau contour bags. These were simply large bags made like pockets, and they were worn on special occasions. They were usually entirely covered with beadwork that consisted of a floral design. Even the background of the bag was completely filled in with beads.

The fourth area includes the tribes of coastal Oregon, Washington, and British Columbia. Here floral beadwork was largely done in an outline design with the background cloth allowed to show through the design. Motifs were not as realistic in appearance and gave only the slightest hint of being floral.

The last major area of floral beadwork covers the Athapaskan speaking tribes of Northwestern Canada. Included with this group are the Metis people of Canada. Metis people are the result of marriages between native Indian women and European men. Originally, these men were involved in the fur trade. There were many of these unions in the area south and west of Hudson Bay, Canada. These people became a culturally and ethnically distinct population. They were middlemen between the native populations and the Europeans.

Metis women began to use floral designs in silk thread embroidery and beadwork around the middle of the nineteenth century. Their floral designs reflected the designs brought by the French, English, Scottish, Swiss, German, Scandinavian, Eastern European, and Russian fur traders, trappers, and settlers.

The Hudson Bay Company and the Roman Catholic mission schools were to a large extent responsible for the spread of and teaching of floral bead embroidery across northwestern Canada. Among the Athapaskan speaking people of this region, it was the custom for females to be in seclusion during puberty and thereafter during their monthly menstrual cycle. During this time young girls practiced their handiwork, including beadwork. Being skilled in the domestic arts was a trait desired in a potential wife.

In none of the five major regions is beadwork as common as it was in the past. This craft does not provide the worker with a decent monetary return for her time and skill in producing her craft item. Presently, beaded items are produced for gifts, for dance costumes, for sale, and for church altar hangings.

There is a great variety in the type of beadwork the different Native American tribes produced. It is beautiful to behold and very inspiring for the quilter. The designs in this book try to provide you with a range of designs that can be found in Woodland, Plains, Plateau, and Northwestern beadwork. It is hoped that you will visit museums and look at books to see original examples of these designs.

None of the blocks provided in this book are total copies of a specific piece of Native American beadwork. Rather, I have tried to extract the essence of the Indian designs and have redrawn them into blocks pleasing to quilters. I have also drawn the blocks with beginning appliqué workers in mind. The designs can always be made more complicated through overlapping motifs and adding motifs. The arrangement of the elements on the stems and the specific flower units is very different from the blocks usually associated with Baltimore style appliqué.

~ INTRODUCTION ~

Native American beadwork pieces can provide the quilter with a new source of inspiration for appliqué designs. You can use the designs in this book as they are provided to appliqué lovely floral motif quilt blocks, or you can use the ideas presented to design your own quilt blocks. If you wish to follow the second method, you will create very original and beautiful quilts from the designs and no two need ever be alike. The variations section beginning on page 34 will explain the design process in more detail. By using some of the embellishment ideas provided, you can give your quilt an even stronger Native American flavor.

Plate 3: Project #1, page 20.

Plate 4.

BASIC APPLIQUÉ TECHNIQUES

Plate 5: Project #2, page 22.

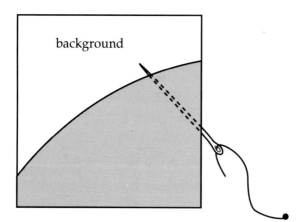

Figure 2.

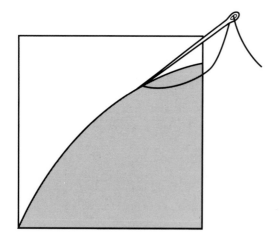

Figure 3.

This book is not meant to provide a detailed description of appliqué techniques. There are a number of excellent books on the market that cover that subject. This section is only a review of some basic techniques needed for these designs.

Finger Pressing

Finger pressing a seam down is an alternative to taking your fabric to an ironing board and ironing the seam. Since I use 100 percent cotton fabrics in my appliqué work, I find the finger press method to be quick and successful. Fold the seam allowance to the back on the pencil marking for the stitching line. Hold the appliqué piece in your right hand, then using the fingernail of your left thumb push against your forefinger and pull the fabric with light pressure across your fingernail.

This creases the fabric on the stitching line and you are ready to sew the motif on the background fabric. Since motifs are going to have some form of bias edge, crease the fabric with care. Be careful not to pull and stretch the motif while you are creasing the seam allowance mark. Otherwise, you will pull the motif out of shape and distort it.

Needle Turn Method

If your motif pieces are very small, using the needle turn method instead of finger pressing gives excellent results. Use a straight pin to hold the motif in place on your background. Start your appliqué stitch and use the point of the needle to push the seam allowance underneath the motif right before you do each stitch. As you push the seam under with the needle, your fingers on your left hand can hold it in place. Usually, after you have taken a few stitches, you can remove the straight pin to get it out of your way.

Appliqué Stitch

Draw your templates for the designs on template plastic. Cut out the plastic without any seam allowances. Trace the shape of the template onto your fabric using whatever type of washout marking device you prefer. I use Dixon® washout cloth markers in blue or red. But I also like Berol Verithin® pencils in silver or white.

Allow a scant ¼ inch seam when cutting your motifs out of the fabric. On the smaller pieces, allow only ⅛ inch seam allowance. On larger pieces of appliqué work, I finger press the entire seam and then stitch the flower down with the basic appliqué stitch.

Once the seam line of the motif has been finger pressed, pin the motif in place on the background fabric. Thread the needle with a color thread that closely matches the color of the motif being sewn. Bring the needle up from under the background and motif. Catch just the outside edge of the piece to be appliquéd (Figure 2). This means you will be catching only a thread or two. Pull your needle up through the layers.

Return the tip of the needle down into the background fabric right next to the hole from which it just came up (Figure 3). About ¹⁄₁₆ of an inch to the left of where the needle just went down, aim the tip of the needle back up through the background fabric and into the appliqué. Catch a thread of the appliqué and pull the needle through the fabric (Figure 4).

Start the needle back down into the background fabric opposite where it just came up. Your stitch should be barely visible (Figure 5). Stitch size and spacing are exaggerated on the drawings.

Curves

Concave curves must be clipped in the seam allowance area to allow them to be sewn down smoothly. Clip about every ⅛ inch just up close to your marking for the seam allowance. Do not cut into the seam allowance (Figure 6). If the curve is relatively gentle, just proceed to sew as you would for regular straight line appliqué. However, if the curve is very sharp and narrow, there are some special adjustments you must make in your stitching.

One cut will have to made right at the center point of the sharp curve. Use a tiny drop of Fray Check® in the

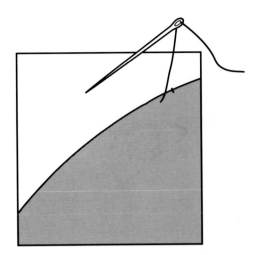

Figure 4.

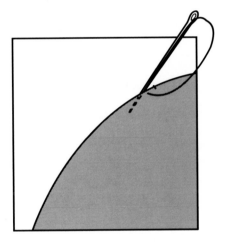

Figure 5.

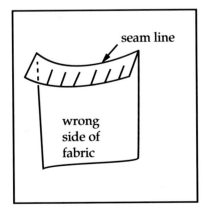

Figure 6.

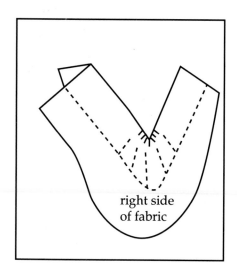

Figure 7.

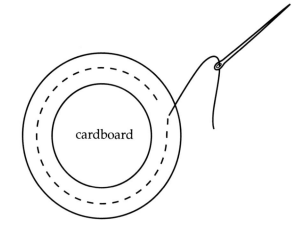

Figure 8.

fabric pulled up
around cardboard
Figure 9.

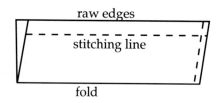

raw edges

stitching line

fold

Figure 10.

area of the "V" point. Also when you are sewing this down, your stitches must be right next to one another as soon as you get to about ⅛ inch from the "V" point. They must stay practically on top of one another until you are out of the curve about ⅛ inch. These two techniques should stop any raveling that might occur. Figure 7 shows the clipping as you would see it if you could see through the fabric to the wrong side of the appliqué. The stitches are on the right side of the motif.

Circles

Instead of making your template for circles out of plastic, cut them out of pieces of lightweight cardboard. Use this to draw your circle on the fabric. Knot a piece of thread and on the right side of your fabric, baste all around the edge of the circle. Try to make the basting stitches in the middle of the seam allowance. Do not tie off the thread yet (Figure 8).

Place your cardboard template on the wrong side of the fabric and pull the thread tight, gathering it around the cardboard. Now make a knot in the fabric to secure the thread. Iron the fabric circle, cardboard and all (Figure 9). I add a little moisture when ironing. A damp press cloth works well.

Let this cool and be sure it is completely dry. Then you can cut the basting thread in one spot and pull out the piece of cardboard. Sew your circle in place.

Stems

I use bias bars for making most of the stems on these designs. I use the ¼ inch size. I cut my stem fabric on the bias, a scant 1 inch wide. Sew the fabric wrong sides together with a full ⅛ inch seam. When the sewing is complete, insert your bar and iron it. This gives you a ¼ inch bias stem strip. When I construct a block, I sew the stems in place first. I pin the stem pieces in place on the background block.

If you have a curved stem, sew the inside curve down first. In most cases, the end of a stem is covered with an appliqué motif or it is secured underneath an intersecting stem. The short stem branches have their outside end turned under ¼ inch and sewn down.

The very narrow stems on the miniature blocks are not made with bias bars. For this stem, cut a piece of bias fabric ¾ inch wide. Crease this in half with an iron (Figure 10). Pin this in place on your stem line. Using a small running stitch, sew it to the background fabric close to the unfolded edge. When this is completed, fold the fabric again so the folded edge just covers the raw edge (Figure 11). Then sew both edges down with an appliqué stitch.

Points

Once your motif with a point has been drawn on fabric, cut it out leaving your usual scant ¼ inch seam allowance. Then square off the long narrow seam allowance and leave a full ⅛ inch seam allowance (Figure 12). Using the finger press method, press the top over and then press first one side (Figure 13) and then the other along the edge of the motif (Figure 14). When sewing on a motif with a point, do not start right at the point. Start about ¼ inch away from the point and sew into the point. Make one stitch at the point and then continue around (Figure 15).

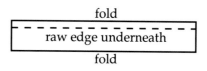

Figure 11.

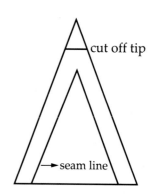

Figure 12.

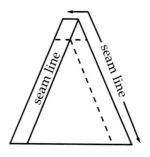

Figure 13.

Figure 14.

Figure 15.

Plate 6: Project #3, page 23.

TYPES OF BEADWORK DESIGNS

It would be very time consuming to discuss the differences and similarities in the beadwork designs among each of the five regions mentioned earlier. However, it is the Northeast Woodland region that provides the greatest number of specimens of floral beadwork for quilters to study. Most of my generalizations about the designs and color schemes are based on this area. Please remember that this is not intended to be a definitive set of statements on Native American floral beadwork. Such research would require extensive studies of museums' collections. However, I have looked at several hundred examples of floral beadwork, and I have noted the following traits that are applicable in the translation of beadwork motifs to appliqué quilt designs.

First, beadwork was often applied to navy, red, black, or brown velveteen or wool fabric. A light color background fabric was uncommon. This was especially true on older pieces. However, many pieces look as if they have a white/cream background. This is because the entire cloth was covered with white beads, allowing the floral and leaf motifs to stand out. The bead colors used for the flowers and leaves were usually variations of red, blue, white, yellow, gold, green, black, navy, and rose. I did not see purple in any of the designs. The colors that would be used were related to the types of beads available from the trading post. A 1940 report shows the Hudson Bay Company carried 12 colors.

Second, designs do not always exhibit bilateral symmetry. This means if you cut a design down the middle, each half is the same once one side has been flipped over to get the mirror image. Further, on the same item you might have a design with bilateral symmetry; and yet other designs on different parts of the object would show no symmetry. Some scholars have speculated that the bilateral symmetry found usually on the older pieces, may derive from a double curve motif that was used on early birchbark, quill, and beadwork items.

Third, the unique arrangements of the beadwork motifs on the background provide new ideas for quilters. In addition to the specific block patterns provided in this book, the appendix has a series of diagrams showing other possible stem arrangements onto which separate flower motifs may be placed.

Fourth, many motifs do not accurately reflect the way the plants appear in nature. Several types of flowers and leaves can be found on the same stem. Fruits, nuts, pinecones, and flowers can be found together on the same vine. And grape, oak, or maple leaves can also be included with these same motifs. Single flowers are placed, without being connected to a stem or branch, in the main design area. I think the beadworker was more concerned with filling space and perhaps balancing the design than with botanical realities. However, since there were a large number of species represented, the beadworker was very familiar with all the plants in her environment.

Paisley designs (teardrops with a curve) were also mixed in with the floral designs. The paisley shawl came from India to England/Scotland in the mid eighteenth century and became a major fashion piece. The English adventurers and settlers brought the paisley design fabric to North America, and it was adapted by the Indians on their beadwork. It fits in well with the floral designs, and its origin in India was probably botanical.

Outlining the leaf and/or flower design with a double row of beadwork in a contrasting color was the sixth trait of beadwork designs. This was a very widespread concept. For example, the rose petals could be medium rose with light pink outlining beads. But outlining did not always follow a monochromatic scheme. The flower could be pink with a navy outline. There might be more than two rows of outline beads. For instance, you could have a light yellow outlining a dark yellow flower; and then there would be a row of red outline beads and a succeeding row of white beads. This means there were actually a series of three outline colors.

The veins of leaves also were differentiated with different colored beads. Sometimes a design would consist of only one or two rows of beads that served as an outline. The rest of the motif was unbeaded so the background fabric showed through. This was especially common in the Northwest Coast area of the northern United States and Canada.

Once the Indians were able to obtain greater quantities of beads, the entire background area of a design was filled in. The fill beadwork was done with concentric rows of beads following the design outline (very much like Hawaiian style echo-quilting) or with horizontal, vertical, or diagonal rows of beads. A rarer type of background beading consisted of following the outside edge of the main piece of fabric. This resulted in a series of concentric squares. These ideas should be remembered when considering the quilting designs for the wall hanging projects.

Another idea that is somewhat foreign to our views of traditional appliqué designs is that flowers and leaves are not always in proportion to one another or to other flowers in the design. There might be very large, overpowering leaves and then smaller flowers that seem out of place in relation to the leaf size. The main goal of the beadworker was to fill in the blank space of the fabric pieces, especially on items such as bandolier pouches (decorative bags or pockets), dance aprons, and vests.

Usually the motifs appear in a static format. Flowers are just laid down on the fabric, connected to one another by a stem but not touching each other. On occasion, however, motifs are sewn so that there is a huge leaf comprising the main motif, and flowers appear to be laid upon it or emanate from the edge of the large leaf. Another format would have smaller leaves onto which flowers are placed so they appear to be laid upon the leaves. Sometimes leaves are placed parallel to the length of a stem on one or both sides of the stem.

The Indians often used metallic, transparent, and translucent beads. This adds a sparkle to the total design that is often difficult to achieve with fabric.

There is an interesting stem design that shows little spikes emanating from each side of the stem down its entire length. This is very common on floral beadwork from the Plains region. Tendrils are also common on the stems. There can also be short branches off a main stem. Such branches do not end with a flower or leaf motif. The tendrils and short branches are filler units for the total design. They give a balance to the variety of leaves and flowers in the design and break the monotony of all floral motifs.

Looking at the total designs there appear to be two classifications — the massed type, and the light, airy type. Designs of the massed or heavy look have little of the background showing. This seems common on the velvet fabric. The flowers are all placed tightly together.

The light, airy overall design format features flower and leaf units isolated along stems or vines and rarely touching each other. A great deal of background shows, and in most cases the background is filled with solid color beadwork that emphasizes the flowers and leaves of the design.

I illustrate how to transform the light, airy design into a more compact design in the section on using beadwork designs. Your own taste preferences, as well as the amount of appliqué sewing you wish to do on each block, will dictate which format you prefer.

The block designs provided in this book exhibit the ideas described in the previous text. The resulting blocks show a relationship to and continuity with the beadwork designs but are not a direct copy of any one design.

Plate 7: Project #4, pages 24-25.

━ EMBELLISHMENTS FOR APPLIQUÉ ━

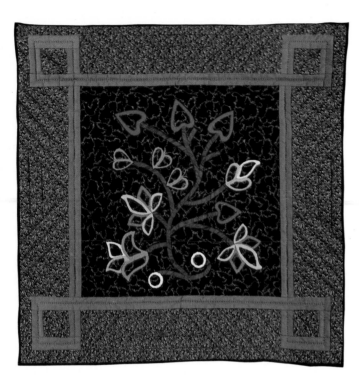

Plate 8: Project #5, pages 26-27.

These techniques give designs a Native American appearance. These methods are relatively easy to do, but they do involve extra time. It is up to each quilter to decide which ideas he or she wishes to try.

Embroidery Stitches

A basic outline stitch applied around the edges of design motifs can be used to duplicate the idea of outlining that was very common on the Native American beadwork. For small blocks, I use two strands of embroidery thread. For sixteen-inch blocks I use three strands. The outline stitch can also be used to form tendrils and leaves. A quilting stitch can be done with embroidery thread to add an entire flower unit. If you enjoy embroidery work, these ideas can be done on all the blocks.

On some stems a straight stitch was used up and down the entire length of the stem (Project #2 detail). This type of stem with spikes was often found on Native American beadwork pieces.

Beads

There are a number of ways of using beads on your quilted project. Beads "by the yard" can be used effectively to outline appliqué pieces. They can replace embroidery. These beads are easy to use. They are molded together so you can cut between beads anywhere, and there is no problem with other beads falling off the string. However, these beads are not as tiny as seed beads, and do not fit well around narrow points. The string of beads is held to your base fabric with couching stitches every two or three beads. If you want beads to go around sharp points, string seed beads on one thread and sew this string in place with a couching stitch done with a second thread.

Another use of beads is as part of fringe on the wallhangings. Miniature Block K shows longer beads strung on monofilament bead thread. The length of the bead string is three inches. Both ends of the monofilament thread are knotted together so that a loop is formed. This loop is then used as fringe on the bottom of a block. Larger size beads called pony beads can be strung on

Plate 9: Project #2, detail, page 22.

yarn fringe that is knotted at the end. Block A (page 35) has this fringe.

A beaded star is made by using eight long tubular beads sewn down on the background fabric. A seed bead is then sewn in the center of this star like motif. Project #10 (page 33) uses these stars as filler units. More detail is given in the section on the sixteen-inch blocks.

Ribbon

A flower made of three short pieces of ribbon duplicates an embellishment idea found on Native American beadwork. The pieces of ribbon are two inches long. Grosgrain ribbon was used so the flowerette stays somewhat stiff looking. However, ethnic examples usually employ satin ribbon so the ends curl up with the passage of time. These ribbon pieces are held in place with a large bead such as a pony bead. The border on Block P has these ribbon flowers made of gray, red, and navy ½" wide ribbon. A brass bead was often used in the center flowers in Native American examples.

Fringe

Project #4 (page 15) uses fringe made from narrow strips of ultra suede scraps. At the end of each fringe is a tin cone jingle. A knot keeps the jingle from coming off. Tin cone jingles were often used on ceremonial clothing as well as beaded objects. Dancers like the way the jingles hit together as the fringe sways with the slightest movement. Sources for the jingles and beads are given in the appendix.

It pays to look around your favorite fabric shop for other ideas for embellishments. Depending on the current design trends, you can find ribbons and trim with Native American designs. Conchos can also be found at stores all over the United States at present because of the interest in Santa Fe clothing and decorating ideas. Although conchos will not be seen on older pieces of floral beadwork sewn by Native Americans, this does not mean they should not be used as decorative devices on your appliquéd wall hangings. These wall hangings are meant to be projects on which you can try a wide variety of embellishment ideas.

Plate 10: Project #6, page 28.

Plate 11: Block P, no pattern provided.

USING BEADWORK DESIGNS

Plate 12: Project #7, pages 29.

Plate 13: Project #8, pages 30-31.

The design pieces used for the blocks are drawn with ease of sewing in mind. Pieces are large in size; curves are gentle; points are tapered. And the total design of the block can be quickly adapted to accommodate more or less appliqué as your personal preference and skill dictate. The majority of my blocks have been hand appliquéd but do not hesitate to use your machine if you wish.

Where there might be confusion as to sewing order, pieces are numbered and brief descriptions are provided.

My husband was instrumental in proposing an idea I want to share with you about proportions of flowers/leaves in the block. He suggested to me that I enlarge the size of the floral motifs so that they really filled a block. He felt this idea resembled closely the ideas that the Native American beadworkers had sometimes used in their designing. I tried the idea in both the miniature and sixteen inch blocks with very pleasing results.

Several blocks in this book show a contrast between normal size as I originally drew them and the enlarged format. There is a greater discussion of this in the Variation sections.

Blocks and borders are interchangeable. The border units are drawn to fit around a sixteen inch (finished size) block. A single block with a border makes a wallhanging that is about 24" square. You can put four blocks together and your wall hanging size will increase to about 40" square. There is one larger four block unit shown in the book. Adding sashing can also increase the size of the finished piece. Just remember to adjust the border pieces to compensate for this.

Preparing the Base Fabric

Decide on your background block color. When selecting your background fabric, remember that if you use a very dark background and then appliqué light colored fabric motifs on it, you may need to put a second piece of fabric as an interlining to keep the background from showing through. Cutting out the background fabric from behind the design can also eliminate this problem. As a general rule I do not cut out my background fabric, but this is really a matter of personal preference.

These blocks are 16" square finished size, which means a 16½" square with seam allowances added. However, cut your background block 17" square to allow for shrinkage in size from the sewing. Once your appliqué and trim work (if you choose to add any embellishments) are done, trim the block back to 16½", being careful to center your design. When you trace the pattern quadrants, make certain all contain a center hash mark to help with centering.

Draw your full-size pattern onto a 16" x 16" piece of freezer paper.

You must draw the design on the waxed side in the case of a non-symmetrial block. If you do not do this, the design will be reversed when you redraw it on your fabric. For a block whose design has bilateral symmetry, draw the design on the unwaxed side of the freezer paper. In either case, iron your freezer paper onto the wrong side of the background fabric. This provides stability for your fabric as you draw the design on it.

Redraw your design on the fabric using a washout marker such as a Dixon® washout pencil.

If you choose to use one of the extra stem arrangements provided, you will need to re-draw it to full size. You can use a copy machine to accomplish this.

Choose your fabrics for the stems and flower/leaves. Sew the stems onto the background first. Be sure you sew them on with a thread that matches the stems as closely as possible. In the case of tendrils where the bias strips form a circle, sew the inside edge of the curves first.

Make templates for the flower elements, allowing *no* seam allowance on the template. Using the template, draw around it on the right side of your fabric. Be sure you use a wash-out pencil or marker for this. Cut out the fabric pieces allowing a scant ¼" seam allowance. You just eye this in. If you are only going to make a block once, you can even use paper for your templates.

Plate 14: Project #9, page 32.

Plate 15: Project #10, page 33 .

PROJECT #1

22" x 22" (Center block 16" x 16")
Border templates on pages 21
Color photo on page 9

Cut:

Block appliqué pieces using
    patterns on pages 44-45

1 – 17" x 17" background square

32 – dark brown triangles
    (Template A)

4 – 1¼" x 45" gold strips

4 – 1¼" x 45" med. brown strips

32 – triangles (Template A, cut
    from strip-pieced fabric)

4 – gold strips (Template K)

4 – gold squares (Template J)

4 – med. brown squares
    (Template J)

4 – 1½" x 22" dark brown strips

Project #1 – Sewing Order

The pattern for the block shows the sewing order on some of the separate motifs. For the row of heart-type designs, sew #1 first. Its center edge and bottom edge are not turned under. Element #2 is laid over the center edge and element #3 is laid over the bottom edge. Proceed with the entire row of hearts this way until you reach the center. Then repeat the process from the left side.

The flower bud shows the sewing order with piece #1 sewn in place first. Only the top point is formed and sewn. The bottom point is formed as pieces #2 and #3 are laid down and sewn in place.

The sewing order is given for the flower at the bottom of the block. For the other blocks in the book the sewing order is not given unless without it there would be some confusion in the appliqué process.

The border design for this block uses a template for a 2" right angle triangle (Template A). (Triangle templates do not include seam allowances.) If you have an Easy Angle®, just cut a 2½" strip of dark brown and cut out 32 triangles (Figure 16). Otherwise, use the template in this book. If you are going to cut the final 1½" border and the binding of this fabric, you will need ½ yard of this fabric.

Cut a strip of gold 1¼" wide and a strip of medium brown print 1¼" wide. Sew these together. You will need four strips of each color if using 45" wide fabric. Place your template A as shown in the drawing (Figure 17) and cut 32 triangles. You will note there is wastage on the strip. Sew these strip pieced triangles to your dark brown triangles to form a square. Sew eight of the squares together. Repeat this so you have four strips each consisting of eight squares.

Sew a strip of these squares on the top of the block and another on the bottom of the block. Construct the four corner blocks. Using your rotary cutter and plastic ruler, cut four gold strips Template K. Also cut four gold squares Template J.

Then cut four medium brown squares Template J. Sew the gold and medium brown print squares together. Add the gold strip (Figure 18).

Sew one of these squares on each corner of the remaining side strips. Check the photograph for placement. Sew these to the sides of the block.

Add a final border of dark brown. Cut each strip 1½" x 22" (extra length is allowed). Trim as needed. The corners are not mitered.

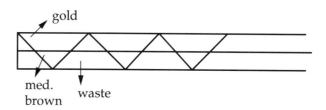

Figure 16.

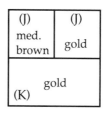

Figure 17.

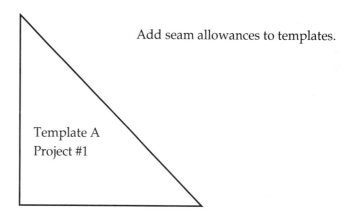

Figure 18.

Add seam allowances to templates.

Template A
Project #1

Template J
Project #1

Template K
Project #1

PROJECT #2

23" x 23" (Center block 16" x 16")

Border templates on pages 22, 79-80

Color photo on page 10

Cut:

Block appliqué pieces using
  patterns on pages 46-47

1 – 17" x 17" background square

8 – green squares (Template L)

8 green, 36 white, 8 lilac, 8 pink,
  20 peach – triangles (Template B)

8 – 2¼" x 5½" white strips
  (extra length allowed)

4 – 2¼" x 10" pink strips
  (extra length allowed)

Project #2 – Adding "Spikes"

There are no special notations or directions for completing this block except that on the full scale drawing you will see short straight lines drawn down the entire length of both sides of the stems. These duplicate in stitching the addition of tiny white beads along the stems on some pieces of beadwork. They are called spikes. Use a straight stitch with two or three strands of embroidery thread to imitate the effect.

The border directions for this project are also easy. On the diagram above and on the picture on page 10, you will see that the green fabric is a stripe that is matched at the corners with a mitre. If you choose not to use a stripe, replace the two triangles with a 2¼" square (Template L, add seams).

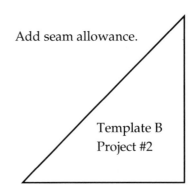

Add seam allowance.

Template B
Project #2

PROJECT #3

26" x 26" (Center block 16" x 16")
Border templates on pages 79-80
Color photo on page 13

Cut:

Block appliqué pieces using
   patterns on pages 48-51

1 – 17" x 17" background square

16 – dark red strips (Template M)

4 dark red, 4 dark blue –
   triangles (Template C)

16 dark blue, 16 light blue,
   16 medium blue, 48 dark red –
   triangles (Template A)

2 – 1½" x 26" dark red strips
   (extra length allowed)

2 – 1½" x 28" dark red strips
   (extra length allowed)

Project #3 – Creating a Fuller Design

This block exhibits the appearance of a heavier, fuller design. There are more motifs on the stem arrangement than is the case with other blocks. If you do not wish this fuller look, subtract some of the separate motifs. Likewise, if you like this particular design format, add motifs to the other blocks. One of the things that makes this block appear fuller is the use of filler elements. These include circles and "S" units. These are not attached to a stem but are placed randomly. These could be used in other blocks in this series as well.

You will need one yard of the block fabric because this is repeated in the border. Dashed lines represent where an outline embroidery stitch was worked. It is placed on top of some appliqué motifs. For the short pieces of stem where one end is not placed under another stem, just turn the end under a scant ¼ inch and sew it down.

For the border, sew a large dark red and large dark blue triangle together. Repeat this four times. Sew the small dark red triangle to a light blue triangle. Sew a dark red triangle to a medium blue triangle. Sew a small dark red triangle to a small dark blue triangle. Repeat this until you have sewn all the triangle units together. Sew two medium blue/red triangle units together for a Flying Geese design. Repeat this process for the rest. Then sew two of these two-triangle units together so one is above the other. Note the placement of the 1½" strip (Template M) between the double triangle units. Follow the diagram and finish the borders.

PROJECT #4

22" x 22" (Center block 16" x 16")
Border templates on page 25
Color photo on page 15

Cut:

Block appliqué pieces using
    patterns on pages 52-55

4 – 6½" squares

2 – 3" x 16½" strips (extra width
    allowed)

2 – 3" x 12½" strips (extra width
    allowed)

4 – 1½" x 16½" gray strips

4 – dark gray squares (Template J)

4 – 2½" x 18½" dark gray strips

4 – light gray squares (Template H)

9 – 4½" strips of Ultra-Suede®

Project #4 – Using Hand Dyed Fabrics

This block is made from hand-dyed fabrics. The main piece of 16½" fabric that composes the background for the block is made of patchwork. There are 4 squares that are 6½" x 6½" (including seams) to which are sewn strips that are 3" x 16½" and 3" x 12½" (including seams). The outside strips are slightly wider and are then trimmed to size after the appliqué work is done. Remember your finished size is a 16½" square onto which the final borders are added.

Cut border strips and squares and sew according to the block diagram. Cut 4 of these. There is an appliqué motif sewn on each corner of the borders (Figure 19).

Along the bottom of the wallhanging there is a border of prairie points and between each point is a fringe of an ultra-suede strip with a tin cone jingle on each end of the fringe. The prairie points are made from a 3" square that is folded in half along the diagonal with the resulting triangle folded in half again (Figure 20). The fringe is a 4½" strip of Ultra-Suede® that is first knotted on one end. A tin cone jingle (source in appendix) is slipped over the knot. Another jingle is threaded on the other end and the end is knotted and the jingle pushed down into the knot (Figure 21). Because of the fringe on the bottom, the wall hanging has a separate binding on only 3 sides.

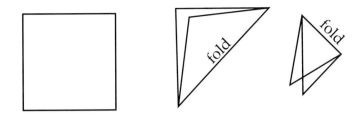

Figure 20.

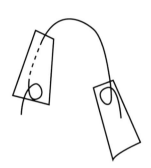

Figure 21.

Add seam allowance to templates.

Template J
Project #4

Template H
Project #4

Figure 19.

PROJECT #5

26" x 26" (Center block 16" x 16")
Border templates on pages 27, 80-81
Color photo on page 16

Cut:

Block appliqué pieces using
   patterns on pages 56-59

1 – 17" x 17" background square

2 – 1½" x 24½" blue strips

8 – green rectangles (Template K)

4 – green rectangles (Template M)

2 – 1½" x 16½" green strips

2 – 1½" x 26½" background fabric strips

2 – 3½" x 16½" background fabric strips

2 – 4½" x 16½" background fabric strips

4 – background fabric squares
   (Template H)

4 – background fabric squares
   (Template J)

4 – background fabric rectangles
   (Template P)

Project #5 – Outlining Appliqué

This block duplicates the beadwork concept of using beads only to outline a design. The background shows through since additional beads are not used to fill in the motifs. To sew this block, the motifs are appliquéd as usual. However, pieces of background fabric are appliquéd on top of these designs, creating the illusion of a design that is only a narrow line of fabric. If you like doing reverse appliqué, that technique would give the same effect.

To assemble the borders, sew a 1½" x 16½" piece to a 4½" x 16½" piece. Repeat and then sew these units to the sides of the block. Next, sew a Template J background square to each end of a 24½" strip (unit 1). Sew two Template K green rectangles to the opposite sides of a Template H square. Repeat this once more. Sew a Tem-

plate M rectangle to the top of this last unit. Repeat. Sew a 3½" x 16½" piece between these two units. Sew a Template P rectangle on either end of this unit (unit 2). Sew unit 1 to unit 2 and then add a 1½" x 26½" piece to the top of this. This completes the top border. Sew it in place. Repeat for the bottom border.

Template H
Project #5

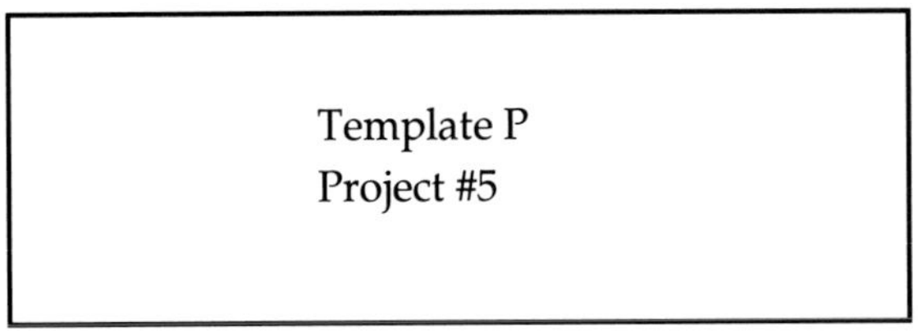

Template P
Project #5

Add seam allowances to templates.

Template K
Project #5

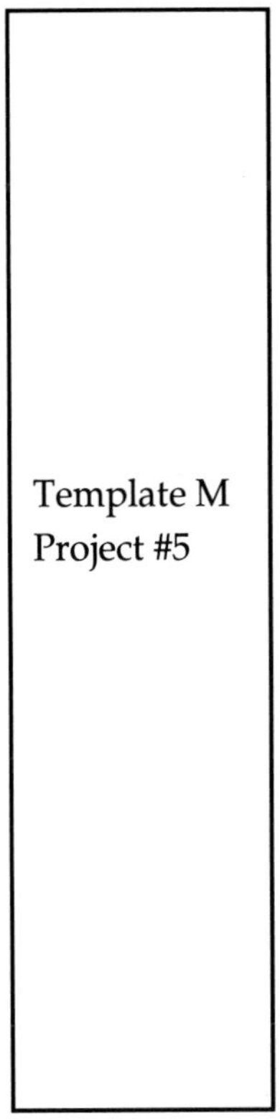

Template M
Project #5

Template J
Project #5

PROJECT #6

24" x 24" (Center block 16" x 16")
Border templates on page 79
Color photo on page 17

Cut:

Block appliqué pieces using
   patterns on pages 60-63

1 – 17" x 17" background square

4 & 4R – blue triangles
   (Template E)

4 & 4R – background fabric
   triangles (Template E)

4 & 4R – background fabric
   triangles (Template D)

4 & 4R – strip-pieced fabric
   triangles (Template C)

4 & 4R – strip-pieced fabric
   triangles (Template D)

8 – 1½" x 45" dark red strips

8 – 1½" x 45" med. red strips

Project #6 – Shadow Appliqué

For this block cut the separate motifs out of the selected fabric (without any seam allowance) and use Wonder Under® to adhere them to the background fabric. Follow the instructions on the particular fusible material you are using.

Cut eight triangles (Template E) from blue and eight from the background fabric. Be sure to reverse half the triangles in each color. To do that, place your template right side up on the fabric for the first four triangles and wrong side up on the fabric for the last four of each color.

Then construct the strip piece border fabric. I used dark red and medium red for the two colors. The strips are 1½" wide (seams included) by your fabric length. If your fabric is 45" in length you will need 2 strips constructed of 4 lengths of fabric for each. Use Template D

to cut your 8 triangles from the strip-pieced fabric and from the background fabric. Again, remember to reverse the templates on one half of the triangles. Eight Template C triangles must also be cut from the strip-pieced fabric.

Once the borders have been sewn together and attached to the appliqué block, cover this entire piece with a lightweight organdy. The organdy lightens the dark reds to pinks. Quilt through the organdy. Be sure to quilt right next to the outside edge of every appliqué piece. Then quilt on the inside edge (about ⅛" from the edge) on every piece. This quilting secures the organdy and causes the designs to puff up. Add other quilting lines as you desire. Also note on the block diagram that there is a flower quilted with red embroidery thread. This is indicated with dashed lines on the drawing.

PROJECT #7

24" x 24" (Center block 16" x 16")
Border templates on page 29, 80
Color photo on page 18

Cut:

Block appliqué pieces using
   patterns on pages 64-65

1 – 17" x 17" background square

4 – purple rectangles
   (Template N)

4 – purple squares (Template H)

4 – beige squares (not the same
   beige as the background)
   (Template H)

4 & 4R – navy triangles
   (Template G)

4 & 4R – blue/green triangles
   (Template G)

8 & 8R – beige triangles
   (Template G)

Project #7 – Outlining

This block has one set of flowers where there are tiny pieces appliquéd inside the main flower petals. This is marked on the block diagram. This technique duplicates the effect of outlining a flower with a color or shade of beads different than the main color of the flower. This design could also be executed in the reverse appliqué technique.

The border is easy to put together. Just look at the picture and block diagram.

Template N
Project # 7
Add seam allowance.

PROJECT #8

24" x 24" (Center block 16" x 16")
Border templates on pages 79-80, 82
Color photo on page 18

Cut:

Block appliqué pieces using
    patterns on pages 66-67

1 – 17" x 17" background square

4 – 2½" x 12½" constructed fabric
    strips

16 – constructed fabric triangles
    (Template A)

4 – constructed fabric strips
    (Template Q)

8 – constructed fabric triangles
    (Template R)

4 – black squares (Template H)

4 – 2½" x 12½" black strips

20 – black triangles (Template A)

8 – black triangles (Template R)

Project #8 – Using Constructed Fabric Background

The designs for this block are appliquéd on a constructed fabric consisting of tiny pieces of hand-painted fabric sewn together. As no foundation fabric is used, there can be a tendency for the pieces to stretch, so be careful not to handle this background too much. After sewing the pieces of fabric together cut a 17" background square for the appliqué. Sew another piece of constructed fabric from which you can cut the remaining patchwork pieces for the border.

The vine section that is appliquéd on the border is made with a Celtic bar in the same width fabric as the stems. A drawing (Figure 22) is given that shows the placement. In most cases you will need to sew several pieces of bias fabric together to make a continuous length. A flower is also added to the border design (Figure 23).

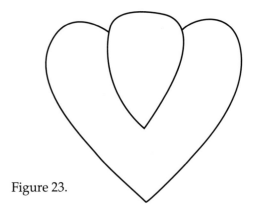

Figure 23.

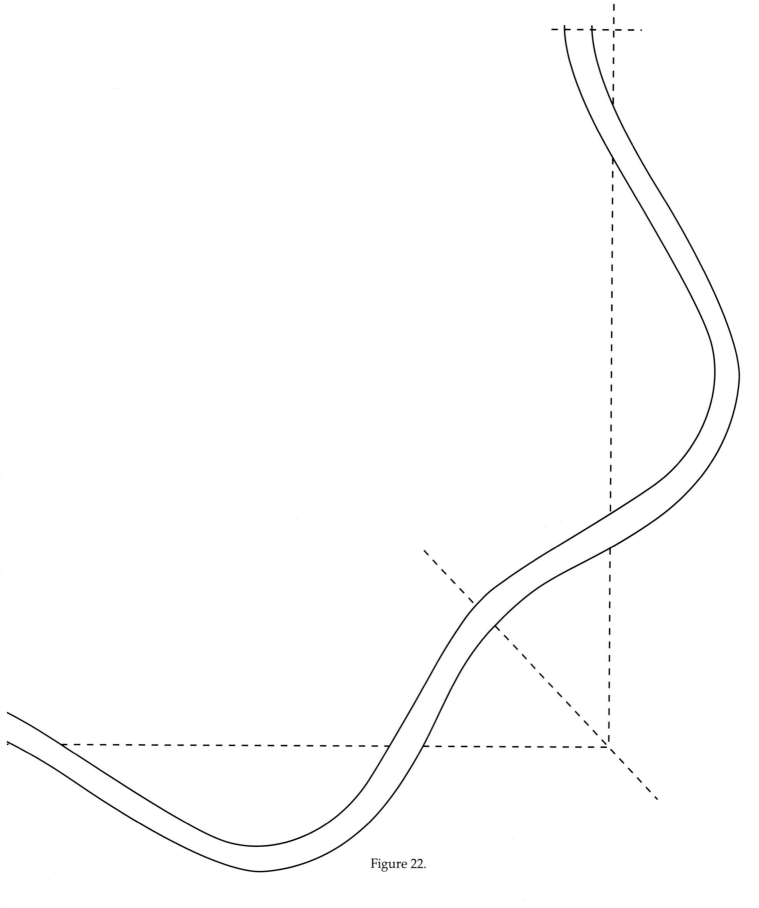

Figure 22.

PROJECT #9

48" x 48"

Border templates on page 81

Color photo on page 19

Cut:

Block appliqué pieces using
   patterns on pages 68-75

4 – 17" x 17" background squares

4 – navy triangles
   (Template Y)

4 – light blue triangles
   (Template Y)

8 & 8R – navy triangles
   (Template Z)

16 & 16R – light blue triangles
   (Template Z)

8 & 8R – red triangles
   (Template Z)

Project #9 – Four Block Wallhanging

This is a four block wallhanging with a finished size of 48" x 48". You can substitute any of the other sixteen inch blocks for the ones used in this example.

The border is 8" wide.

Sew these together according to the master diagram. The pieces are large and the border finishes up in a hurry. In the corners of the border there is a small appliqué flower. This unit is taken from Project #5.

PROJECT #10

24" x 24" (Center block 16" x 16")

Border templates on pages 79-81

Color photo on page 19

Cut:

Block appliqué pieces using
    patterns on pages 76-77

1 – 17" x 17" background square

4 – 1½" x 12½" light gray strips

16 – light gray triangles (Template X)

4 – 1½" light gray squares

16 – mauve triangles (Template X)

16 – beige triangles (Template A)

4 – beige squares (Template H)

4 – 2½" x 10½" beige strips

16 – green triangles (Template A)

8 – rust rectangles (Template P)

16 – rust triangles (Template X)

8 – med. beige triangles (Template X)

4 – 1½" x 12½" med. beige strips

Project #10 – Experimenting with Background Fabrics

The background fabric for this block is a wild print turned to the wrong side so that the colors appear muted. Experimenting with background fabrics that are not solid colors can provide interesting visual excitement to the blocks.

This block uses some embellishments. On the outside edge of some of the flower motifs, beads "by the yard" were sewn down. This is a special type of prestrung beading that has the beads molded together. The beads are easier to sew down since you do not have to hand string each bead. The beads can be easily cut apart at any spot between beads by using a pair of old scissors.

Sewn on the background are star-like beaded motifs.

Each is constructed of 8 bugle beads and 1 seed bead. See Figure 24. They are sewn down by hand once the appliqué is finished and before the layers are put together for the quilting. I just marked 8 lines freehand and then sewed the beads over them. You do not have to be precise with this. The seed bead is sewn down in the center.

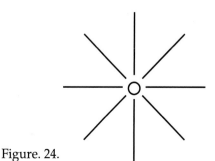

Figure. 24.

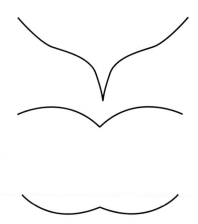

Figure 25.

Figure 26.

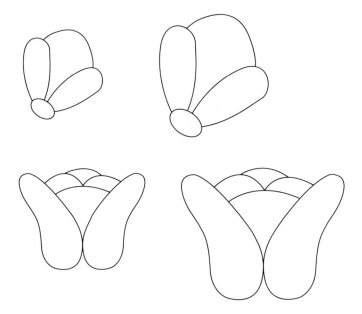

Figure 27.

Once you experiment with some of the specific designs provided, you will probably want to create some designs that are uniquely yours. This chapter shows you some of the ways you can achieve originality in your work. You will find these different processes easy to accomplish and rewarding in their results.

Look at all the blocks pictured in the book. Cover up the borders. Decide which designs appeal to you. Then make some selections from either these blocks or the other options provided in the back of the book.

General Instructions

Use a piece of paper that is 16" square. This does not allow for seam allowances. You can tape two pieces of paper together. First, choose your stem arrangement. Note whether you will want bilateral symmetry, a circular format, or a branching style. Draw your stem arrangement selection on the paper. See pages 90-94 for some examples. Use a pencil to draw and do not mark heavily. If you are using a design with bilateral symmetry, you may wish to fold the paper in half to make this task easier. Mark the stems ¼" wide (Figure 25).

Second, select specific flower and leaf elements you find attractive and within your skill level. See pages 84-89 for examples. Use a light box and add selected flowers and other motifs from the book. It is easiest to copy the pages, cut out motifs, and lay them on the paper. When you copy the pages of motifs, you can enlarge or reduce them as needed. Keep arranging the motifs and adding or subtracting them until you have an arrangement that is pleasing to you. Remember that flowers don't have to be attached to a stem, and different flower types can appear on the same stem. You can also use just sections of a complicated flower design, creating a smaller, simpler unit. If you are doing a bilaterally symmetrical piece, you only need to work on one half of the design. You can simply fold your paper in half and trace the design onto the other half of the paper with the use of a light box (Figure 26).

Add any other designing ideas you may wish. This could include embroidery details or filler elements such as paisleys, circles, short stems, hairs on the stems, etc.

Once you have decided this is a design you love, cut a piece of freezer paper that is 16" square. Draw your design on the non-wax side of the paper. Use a pencil for your initial drawing. Look at the design again to double check that it is pleasing to you. It helps to pin it up against the wall and stand back to view the block. Then draw over all your designs and stems with a black permanent marker. I use one with a fine point. The black ink makes the lines easier to see when you need to transfer the pattern to your fabric.

Since the design is drawn on freezer paper, I can iron the freezer paper to the wrong side of my background fabric. If your design does not have bilateral symmetry it will be reversed with this method. I do not find that this is a problem with any of the projects I have designed. However, it you prefer the design not be reversed, draw on the wax side of the paper. I like the freezer paper because once it is ironed to the background fabric, you can trace your design to the front easily with no slippage of the pattern. Pull it off carefully once you are ready to begin sewing.

Variation #1 – Enlargement

Block A shows how a design looks when it has been enlarged using a copier. This is the same design as Project #10. However, the block looks heavier and fuller. Block C is the same as Block B. This gives you an idea of the appearance you will achieve depending on the degree of enlargement you wish to pursue. Figure 27 shows an example of the size difference between single elements in the separate blocks. I usually start with a 25 percent or 30 percent increase in size. Use the stem arrangement of your normally sized block. Cut out the enlarged separate motifs and place them on the stem. When you are satisfied with the results, glue the elements down. Re-draw the design on good paper if necessary.

This method does result in larger pieces to sew, which may make it easier for you to handle. However, you probably should consider drawing a more massive

Plate 16: Block A.

Plate 17: Project #10, page 33.

Plate 18: Block B, no pattern provided.

Plate 19: Block C, no pattern provided.

looking border for the block. Remember if you choose to do a wall hanging of several blocks, it is better to choose one size and stick with it. Combining blocks of enlarged designs with blocks of smaller designs can create an imbalance in the piece. This is not to say that many of the beadwork pieces did not exhibit flowers that were out of proportion to one another. You can combine large and small flowers in the same block. It is the overall appearance of the block that is important.

Notice the "fingers" (as the Indians called them) hanging from the bottom of the wall hanging (Plate 16: Block A). The appendix has the pattern for the finger. Make the yarn fringe with its pony beads first. Take 6 or 7 strands, about 4" long, of a worsted weight yarn. Tie a knot up about 1¼". Unravel the yarn that short distance. String three pony beads on the tassel. You can trim it to the finished length you want once you are ready to place it in the fabric finger.

For each finger, cut 2 of the patterns out of fabric and 1 out of a thin iron-on interfacing. The interfacing can be ironed to the wrong side of 1 piece of your fabric before sewing. Also place a yarn fringe tassel at the rounded point of the finger before you sew. Sew these right sides together with a ¼" seam, leaving the top open. Turn right side out. Make 5 of these fingers. Space them evenly along the bottom of your wall hanging. Sew the bottom edge of the wall hanging with its backing and batting before you begin quilting. Again sew right sides together with a ¼" seam. Turn the batting and backing up and baste the quilt as you normally would before quilting. When the quilting is finished, binding will only need to be sewn along the top and two sides to finish off the quilt.

Variation #2 – Enlargement and Overlap

Block D shows several ideas taken directly from beadwork pieces. The flowers are enlarged as were the ones in the previous block. However, they were not enlarged to as great a degree. The maple leaf on the pattern looks as through it has been laid on top of other flowers. Overlap occurs on beadwork pieces though not to a great extent. There is also a free floating flower unit above the maple leaf. Motifs on beadwork items can free float with no stem attachments. Since the beadwork pieces used for this project crossed many tribes, geographical boundaries, and time periods, most any design format can be found to have been attempted.

Tiny ribbon was sewn on the maple leaf motif to imitate veins on a natural leaf.

Variation #3 – Fabric Painting

Some of you have a variety of fabric paints on hand left over from sweatshirt projects. If so, consider using them to paint your appliqué design. The results are quite lovely. You can outline designs or shade the paint. This is a much faster technique than hand appliqué, and you can mix any color you want.

Variation #4 – Button Appliqué

On the Northwest Coast there was a type of blanket made that featured white mother-of-pearl buttons sewn to outline a design. This use of buttons was combined with small patches of fabric appliqué to create Block E. If you live near a shirt factory, you can usually purchase large quantities of small white buttons for very reasonable prices. Many of the Northwest Coast blankets were done with a red wool background, so I used that color in this piece. I added white and navy as the accent colors.

When sewing the buttons in place be sure to leave a little space between them so that they will be flat on the fabric. I found it easier to sew the buttons in place if I put a drop of washable glue along the stems and placed the buttons in place on top of this. After the glue had dried I could sew the buttons on without their slipping around. I would only glue about 10 at a time. You can, however, glue and sew on more than one area of the design at a time. Mix the size of buttons used, to add variety to the design.

I have also used an iron-on interfacing on the back of my background fabric. This provides stability as the buttons add weight to the fabric. The drawing for this

Plate 20: Block D, no pattern provided.

Plate 21: Block E, reduced size drawing on page 83.

Plate 22: Block F, no pattern provided.

Plate 23: Block G.

block shows a single line for the stems rather than the double lines ¼" wide in the other drawings. The reason for this is that the size of button you use may vary between ¼" and ⅜" so I felt it would be easier to leave the stems as a line. The lines and general sizes for them are approximate. Just come as close as you can with the size buttons you have to work with. You can use this design for regular appliqué; simply center the bias bar over the straight lines in the drawing.

Variation #5 – Broidere Perse

Block F shows how adapting the technique of broidere perse can also help you create truly unique blocks. This technique involves cutting out flower and leaf motifs from printed fabrics and then appliquéing these onto the background. This allows you to combine many unusual and varied motifs from numerous pieces of fabric into a coordinated whole. You can often find flowers with the centers already printed on them, which saves you a step in the traditional appliqué process.

Remember that with this design, you can mark only the general location of flowers or leaves with an **X**. You will not be using the specific flower shapes given for a design. Your flower pattern will be determined by the flower design you cut from the printed fabric. The fabric also provides texture to the petals and depth to the color by virtue of the printed design.

Variation #6 – Creating a Filled Design

Block G is the same basic design as Project #4. The design is reversed on the background. Most noticeable is that many more elements have been added to the design to greatly reduce the amount of background fabric showing. The motifs were also slightly enlarged for this design.

Variation #7 – White on White Quilting

Block H (adapted from Block D, Project #9) shows how an appliqué design can be used for white on white quilting. The results are lovely. It is best to use a main block design that has many elements, in other words the more massive look. Then select a type of background quilting such as diagonal lines or parallel lines that accents the quilted designs.

Use a colored quilting thread to accentuate the quilted motif.

Variation #8 – Using Appliqué Motifs in Sashing

Block I shows appliqué motifs used in the sashing between four tiny Log Cabin blocks. If you like the appeal of appliqué but do not want to do a lot of it, this method is for you. The winding vine with circles is very quick and easy to sew.

Variation #9 – Outline Embroidery

Block J illustrates a miniature design in which the flowers were taken normal size from a sixteen inch block pattern. This means only a few flowers could be used in the block, thus reducing the amount of appliqué sewing needed. Around the inside edges of the flowers an outline embroidery stitch was done with three strands of embroidery floss. Contrasting colors of thread were used. This imitates the outlining effects of rows of beads.

Plate 24: Block H, no pattern provided.

Plate 25: Block I, no pattern provided.

Plate 26: Block J, no pattern provided.

Variation #10 – Miniature Blocks

Blocks can be made in miniature and used in wall-hangings, individually, or in groups. The 6" blocks are done following the basic instructions provided elsewhere with the full-size blocks.

Block K shows the miniature size motifs utilized in a filled, massive arrangement rather than a light, airy arrangement. The block is finished only with outline quilting around the appliqué units on the block. Parallel lines pointing inward toward the block are on the border. The borders consist of three fabrics. The print fabric is ¾" wide finished size. The turquoise border is ½" wide finished size, and the last border of purple fabric is ¾" wide. On the bottom of the block, the purple border is a gentle curve design to which has been added bead fringe. These turquoise and white beads are each about 1¼" long so they are much larger than seed beads.

To construct the bottom border, cut 2 pieces of the curve design. Cut one of the purple and one of the quilt background fabric. Double-check before you cut to make sure this unit fits your block with the borders added. As you sew the two curved pieces right sides together, place the beaded fringe pieces in the seam. I used tiny pieces of masking tape to hold them in place during the sewing. After the sewing is complete, turn the unit right sides out.

Next, this unit is then sewn onto the main block unit. The batting is pinned in place on the wrong side of the block. Keep your pins on the front side of the block. Fold up ¼" at the bottom of the backing and iron this seam. Keep this ¼" folded up with the use of pins.

Put the backing against the front of the block, right sides together, and sew around the two sides and the top with your ¼" seam. The curved unit has no batting. Turn the piece inside out. The seam from the top of the curved piece fits up under the turned down ¼" of the backing, and this opening is sewn shut with an appliqué stitch.

The Christmas-colored miniature Blocks L - O show how miniature elements look when they are enlarged slightly with a copy machine. Some purists might argue

Plate 27: Block K, page 78.

that they are not truly miniature. But these blocks are made with the same variations employed on the 16" blocks. Whichever method you use will reflect your own personal preferences.

Another idea for the miniature blocks consists of selecting a very simple stem pattern as the basis for the block. You can then place the full size flowers from the 16" blocks on this pattern. Don't enlarge any motifs. We tend to think of the elements in miniature pieces as being small so it takes a mental adjustment to do this. Some of the elements in the 16" blocks are too large but many of them will work for this idea. The block size remains 6" x 6"; but the motifs, being larger in size, fill the block.

Also remember that you can reduce full-size flower elements with a copy machine and use them in miniature blocks. You might have to omit some lines if the design gets too complicated.

The border for the Christmas blocks consists of ½" finished strips of the Christmas print fabric. The off-white fabric in the border is only ¼" finished size. A diagram for the construction is included (Figure 28). Block O also includes some tendrils added to the stems with red embroidery thread in an outline stitch.

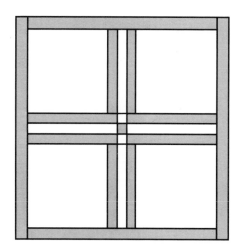

Figure 28.

Plate 28: Blocks L - O. Pattern for Block L, page 43.

QUILTING IDEAS

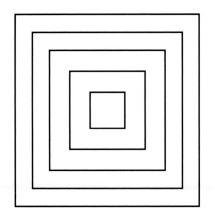

Figure 29.

My first step in quilting an appliqué block is to outline quilt each motif at the very outside edge of the motif. This makes the design puff up. Depending on the design, I might also quilt on the inside of a flower or leaf element. Doing this on larger motifs gives them extra holding power on the background.

Remember quilting lines on a plain background will show up more than will quilting lines on a heavily patterned fabric. Background quilting with parallel lines works to emphasize the appliqué designs. These lines are usually one inch apart. I use masking tape to mark my lines. With the tape I can avoid the use of a pencil. Just remember not to leave the masking tape on your project if you are not coming back to it within a few days. The tape leaves a sticky residue. In one case, Project #1, I used diagonal lines that were two inches apart.

Sometimes I added extra flowers, tendrils, or stems in quilting stitches to the main design. Project #6 shows this with a flower quilted in red embroidery thread. Project #4 has leaves and a curved stem unit in the border. Another type of quilting I like for the blocks is stipple quilting. I find this enjoyable to do since one can just wander anywhere with the stitches. Projects #3 and #4 have this form of quilting.

Projects #5 and #8 have echo quilting. Block A (Plate 16: page 35) shows no background quilting. The design is outline quilted and little "S" shaped filler units are quilted randomly on the surface. These filler quilting units are similar to those navy appliqué filler units found in Project #3. Radiating lines were used in Project #7 (to mimic the radiating appliqué design on the block). Finally, Block P (Plate 11: page 17) uses concentric, though not circular, parallel lines that follow the outside of the block and keep moving toward the center with smaller and smaller squares. Figure 29 shows a diagram of this.

The parallel lines and echo quilting imitate the background beading that is found on many of the original beadwork pieces. Obviously, in some of the beadwork pieces there was no beaded background. The motifs were often beaded on a dark velvet background and the velvet was allowed to show through.

Block L.

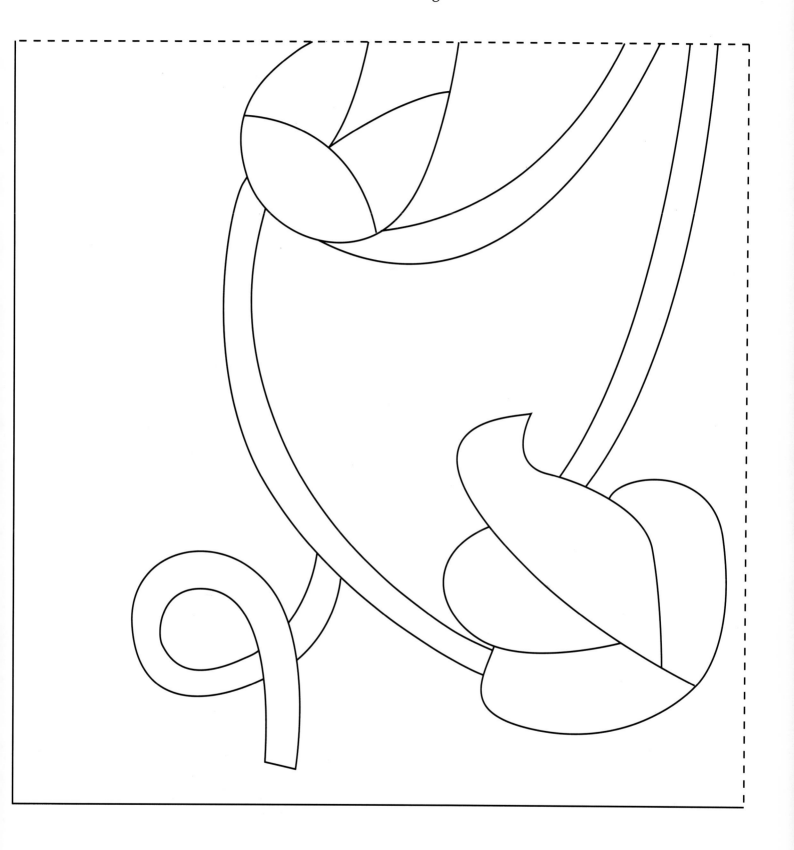

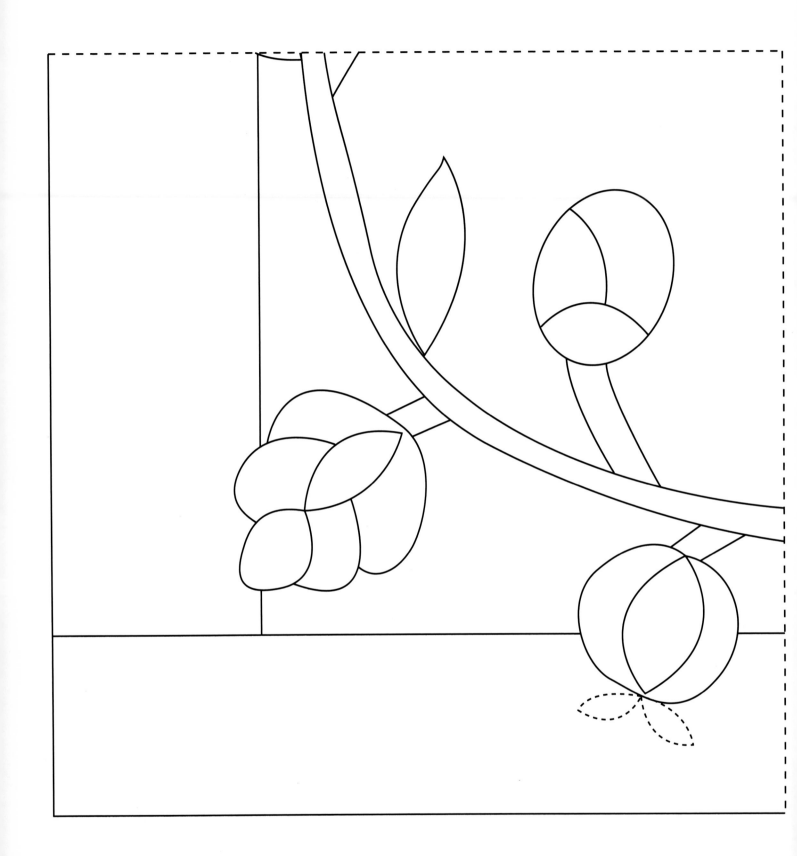

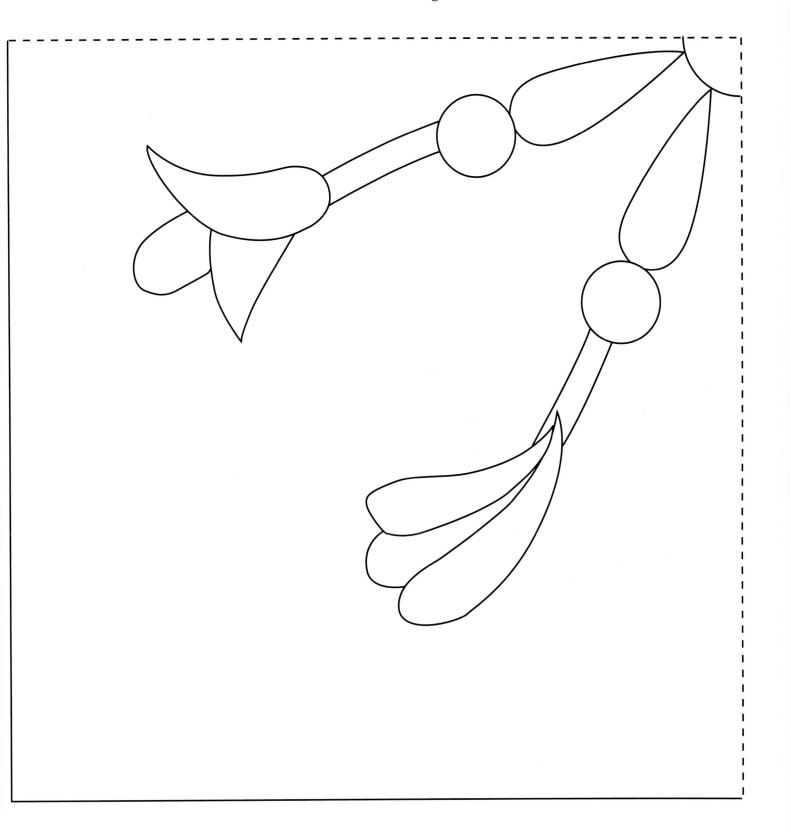

Reverse for Upper Right

Reverse for Lower Right

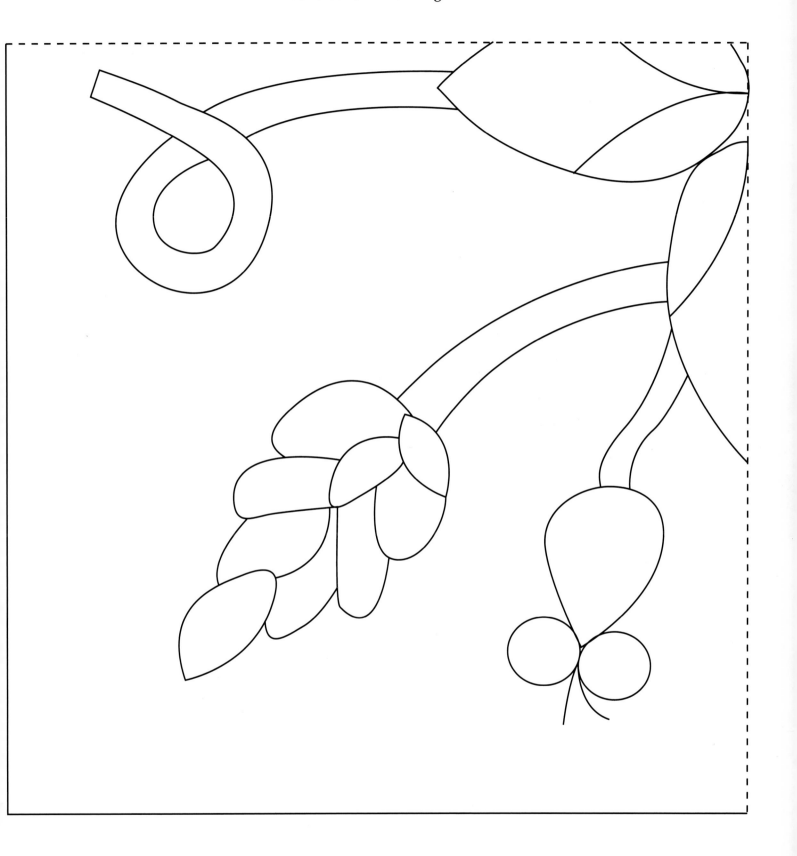

Reverse for Lower Right

Reverse for Upper Right

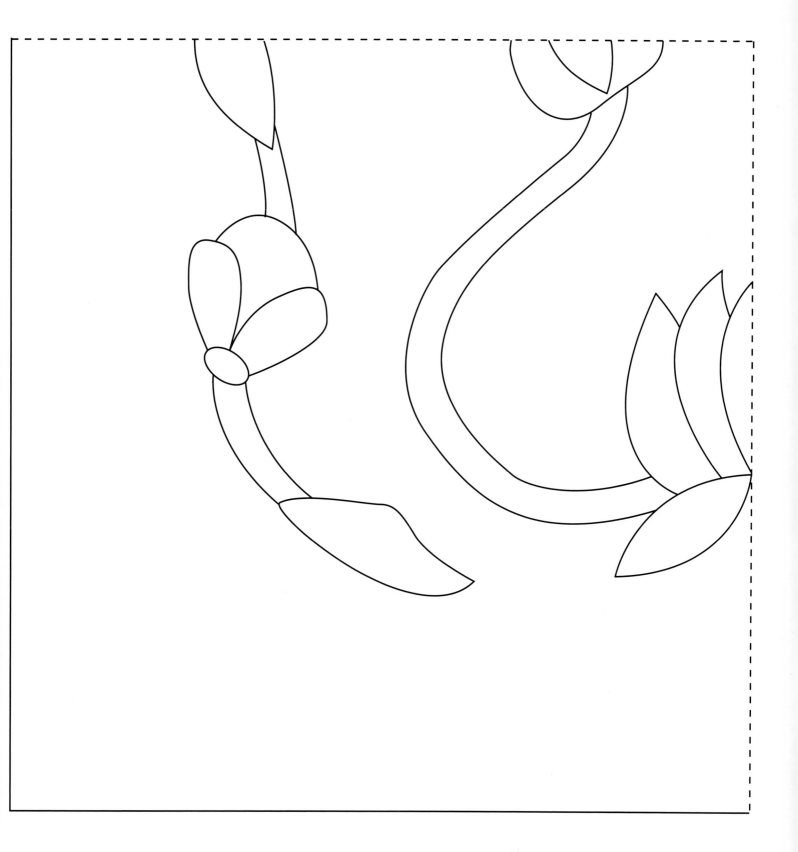

BORDER TEMPLATES

Add seam allowances.

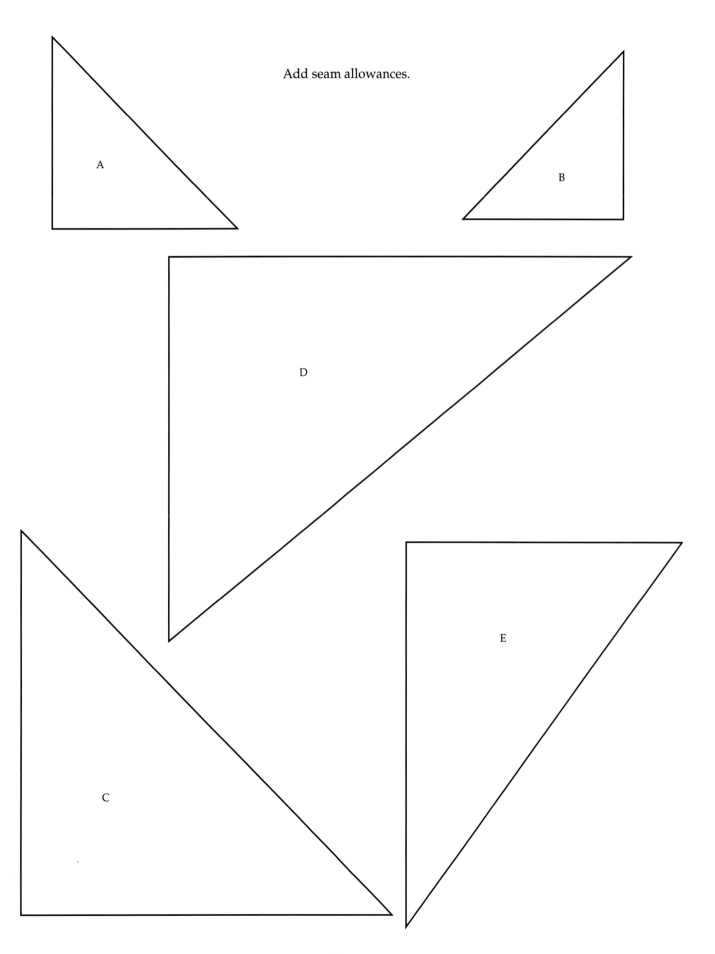

A

B

D

C

E

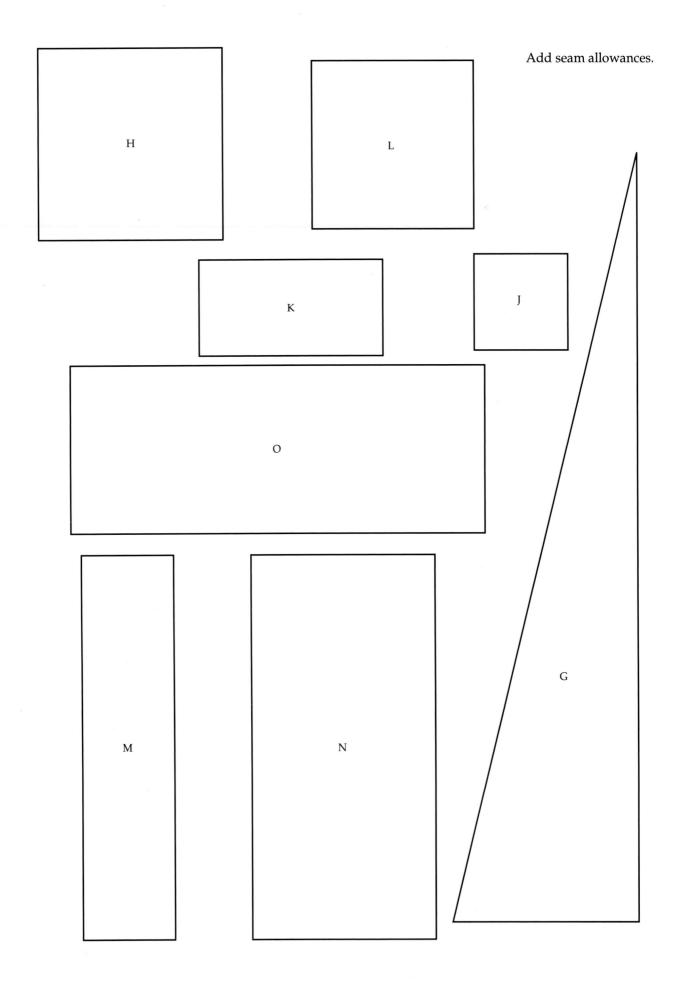

Add seam allowances.

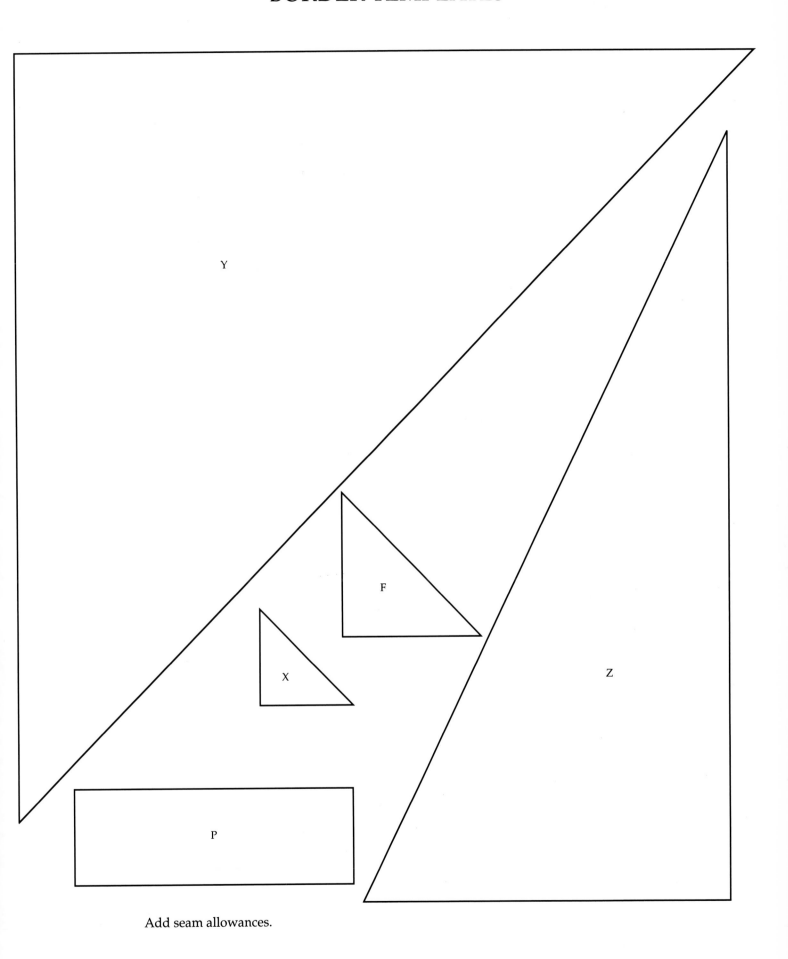

Y

F

X

Z

P

Add seam allowances.

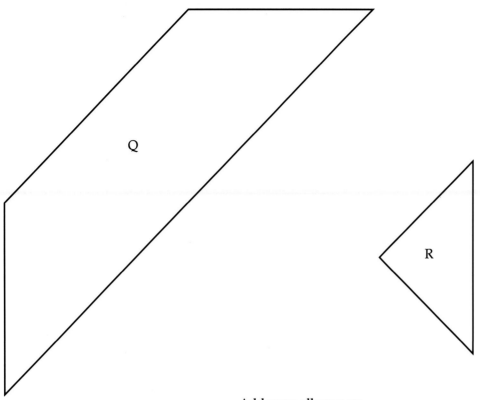

Add seam allowances.

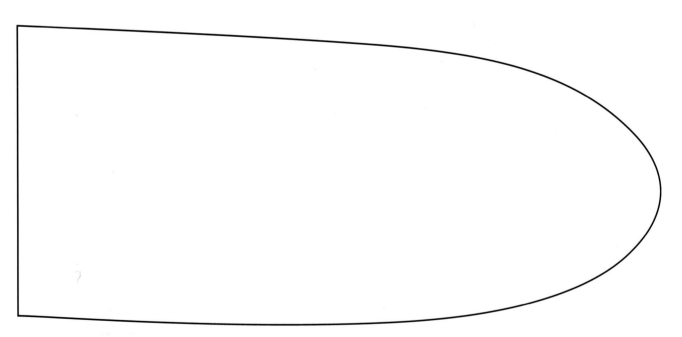

Block A "finger" pattern

FLOWER UNITS

STEM ARRANGEMENTS

In addition to the stem arrangements presented in the examples of the blocks used in the book, this appendix contains over 25 additional ideas. They were taken from beadwork pieces of varying sizes so all of them might not be appropriate for sixteen inch blocks or miniature blocks. Some would work very well on twenty-four inch blocks. They are meant to give you a general guideline for designing new applique blocks. They are included because they are very different in many cases from typical appliqué arrangements seen in quilts.

The X markings indicate placement for large flower motifs as they were placed on the original beadwork pieces. When beginning your design with one of these stem arrangements, it is often easiest to just draw the main stem freehand onto your piece of paper. Add other secondary stems as you see fit. Add your flowers. Your filler circle or S-shapes filler units, if you wish them, are added last. Remember these are fanciful flower arrangements and not botanical renderings for a college textbook.

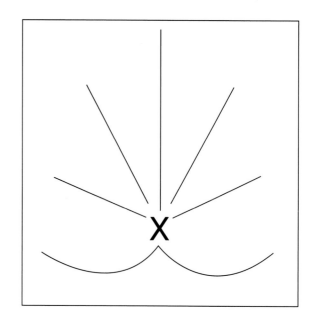

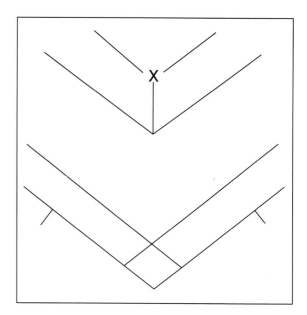

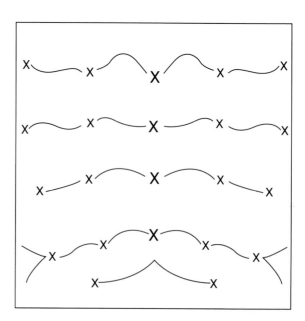

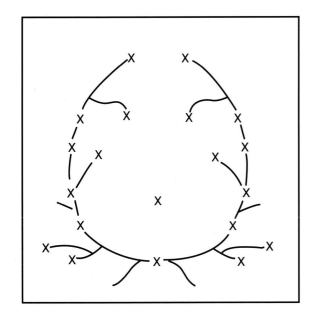

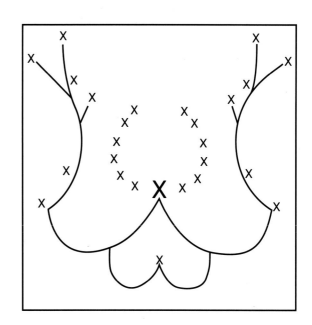

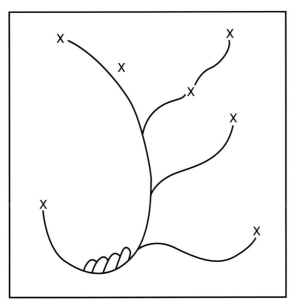

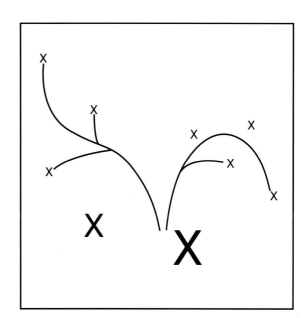

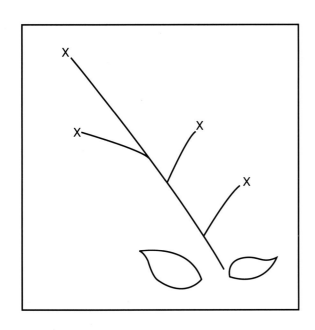

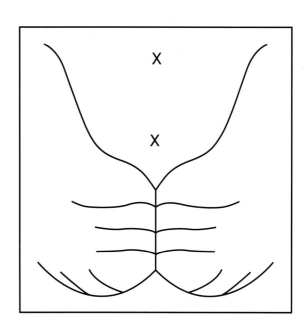

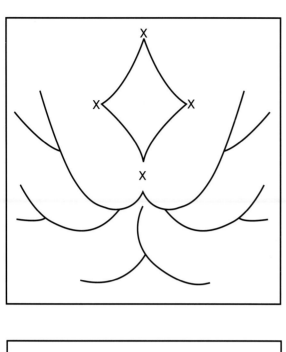

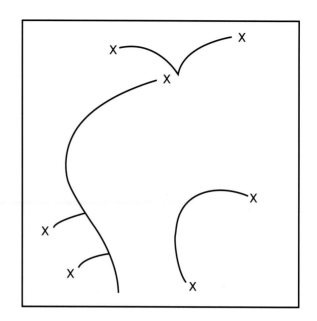

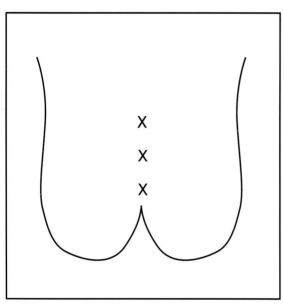

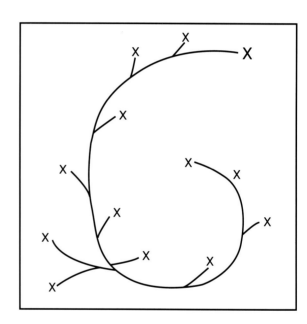

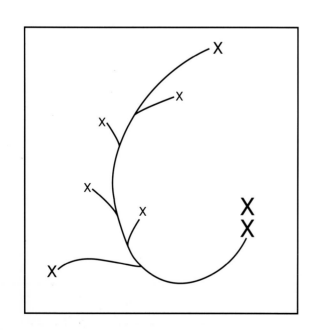

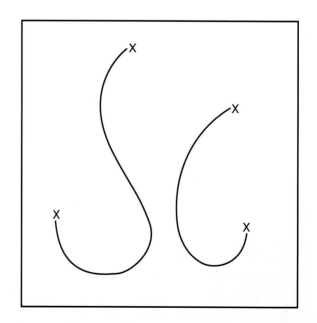

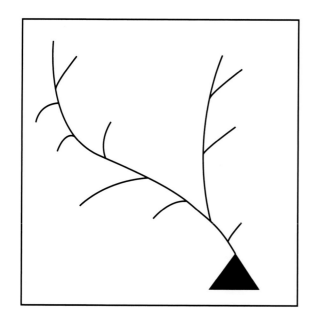

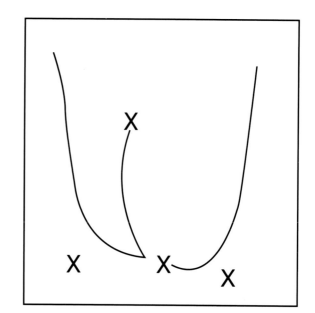

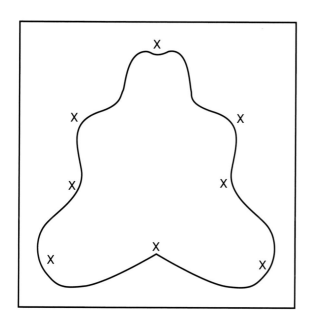

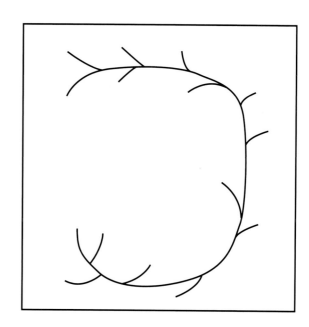

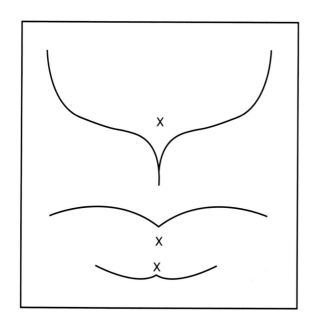

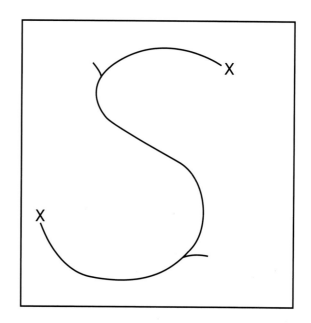

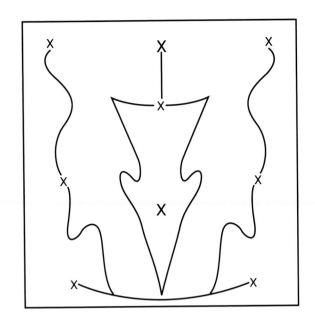

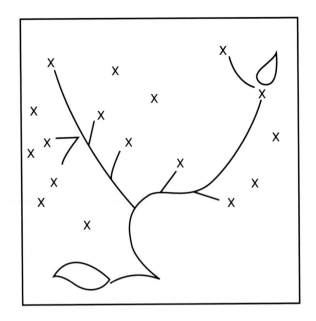

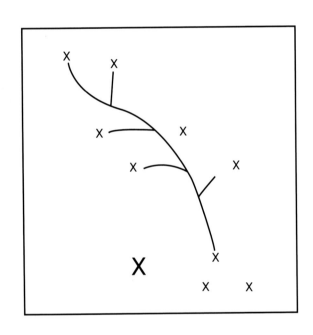

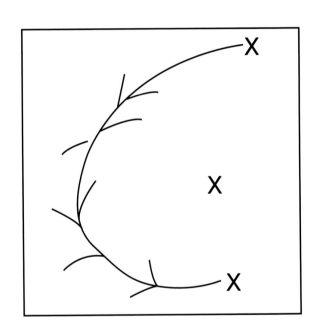

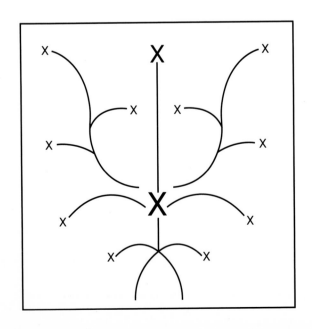

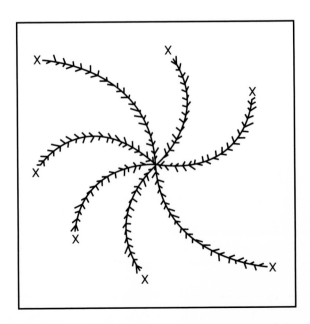

⦈ SUPPLIERS ⦇

Crazy Crow Trading Post
P.O. Box 314
Denison, TX 75020

Eagle Feather Trading Post
168 W. 12th St.
Ogden, UT 84404

Grey Owl Indian Craft Company
113-15 Springfield Blvd.
P.O. Box 507
Queens Village, NY 11429

Western Trading Post
P.O. Box 9070
Denver, CO 80209-0070

⦈ BIBLIOGRAPHY ⦇

Beads: Their Use By Upper Great Lakes Indians. Grand Rapids Public Museum, 1977.

Denver Art Museum Leaflets 117, 118, and 119. Denver, Colorado, n.d.

Kate Duncan. *A Special Gift: The Kutchin Beadwork Tradition.* University of Washington Press, 1988.

Kate Duncan. *Northern Athapaskan Art.* University of Washington Press, 1989.

Barbara Hail. "Out of the North: Subarctic Arts at the Haffenreffer Museum of Anthropology," *American Indian Art Magazine.* Spring, 1991. pp. 68-79.

John Anson Warner. "Continuity and Change in Modern Plains Cree Moccasins," *American Indian Art Magazine.* Summer, 1990. pp. 36-47.

∽American Quilter's Society∾

dedicated to publishing books for today's quilters

The following AQS publications are currently available:

- **Adapting Architectural Details for Quilts,** Carol Wagner, #2282: AQS, 1991, 88 pages, softbound, $12.95
- **American Beauties: Rose & Tulip Quilts,** Gwen Marston & Joe Cunningham, #1907: AQS, 1988, 96 pages, softbound, $14.95
- **America's Pictorial Quilts,** Caron L. Mosey, #1662: AQS, 1985, 112 pages, hardbound, $19.95
- **Applique Designs: My Mother Taught Me to Sew,** Faye Anderson, #2121: AQS, 1990, 80 pages, softbound, $12.95
- **Arkansas Quilts: Arkansas Warmth,** Arkansas Quilter's Guild, Inc., #1908: AQS, 1987, 144 pages, hardbound, $24.95
- **The Art of Hand Applique,** Laura Lee Fritz, #2122: AQS, 1990, 80 pages, softbound, $14.95
- **...Ask Helen More About Quilting Designs,** Helen Squire, #2099: AQS, 1990, 54 pages, 17 x 11, spiral-bound, $14.95
- **Award-Winning Quilts & Their Makers: Vol. I, The Best of AQS Shows – 1985-1987,** #2207: AQS, 1991, 232 pages, softbound, $24.95
- **Award-Winning Quilts & Their Makers: Vol. II, The Best of AQS Shows – 1988-1989,** #2354: AQS, 1992, 176 pages, softbound, $24.95
- **Award-Winning Quilts & Their Makers: Vol. III, The Best of AQS Shows – 1990-1991,** #3425: AQS, 1993, 180 pages, softbound, $24.95
- **Classic Basket Quilts,** Elizabeth Porter & Marianne Fons, #2208: AQS, 1991, 128 pages, softbound, $16.95
- **A Collection of Favorite Quilts,** Judy Florence, #2119: AQS, 1990, 136 pages, softbound, $18.95
- **Creative Machine Art,** Sharee Dawn Roberts, #2355: AQS, 1992, 142 pages, 9 x 9, softbound, $24.95
- **Dear Helen, Can You Tell Me?...All About Quilting Designs,** Helen Squire, #1820: AQS, 1987, 51 pages, 17 x 11, spiral-bound, $12.95
- **Dye Painting!,** Ann Johnston, #3399: AQS, 1992, 88 pages, softbound, $19.95
- **Dyeing & Overdyeing of Cotton Fabrics,** Judy Mercer Tescher, #2030: AQS, 1990, 54 pages, softbound, $9.95
- **Encyclopedia of Pieced Quilt Patterns,** compiled by Barbara Brackman, #3468: AQS, 1993, 552 pages, hardbound, $34.95
- **Flavor Quilts for Kids to Make: Complete Instructions for Teaching Children to Dye, Decorate & Sew Quilts,** Jennifer Amor #2356: AQS, 1991, 120 pages, softbound, $12.95
- **From Basics to Binding: A Complete Guide to Making Quilts,** Karen Kay Buckley, #2381: AQS, 1992, 160 pages, softbound, $16.95
- **Fun & Fancy Machine Quiltmaking,** Lois Smith, #1982: AQS, 1989, 144 pages, softbound, $19.95
- **Gallery of American Quilts 1830-1991: Book III,** #3421: AQS, 1992, 128 pages, softbound, $19.95
- **The Grand Finale: A Quilter's Guide to Finishing Projects,** Linda Denner, #1924: AQS, 1988, 96 pages, softbound, $14.95
- **Heirloom Miniatures,** Tina M. Gravatt, #2097: AQS, 1990, 64 pages, softbound, $9.95
- **Infinite Stars,** Gayle Bong, #2283: AQS, 1992, 72 pages, softbound, $12.95
- **The Ins and Outs: Perfecting the Quilting Stitch,** Patricia J. Morris, #2120: AQS, 1990, 96 pages, softbound, $9.95
- **Irish Chain Quilts: A Workbook of Irish Chains & Related Patterns,** Joyce B. Peaden, #1906: AQS, 1988, 96 pages, softbound, $14.95
- **Jacobean Appliqué: Book I, "Exotica,"** Patricia B. Campbell and Mimi Ayars, Ph.D., #3784: AQS, 1993, 160 pages, softbound, $18.95
- **The Log Cabin Returns to Kentucky: Quilts from the Pilgrim/Roy Collection,** Gerald Roy and Paul Pilgrim, #3329: AQS, 1992, 36 pages, 9 x 7, softbound, $12.95
- **Marbling Fabrics for Quilts: A Guide for Learning & Teaching,** Kathy Fawcett & Carol Shoaf, #2206: AQS, 1991, 72 pages, softbound, $12.95
- **More Projects and Patterns: A Second Collection of Favorite Quilts,** Judy Florence, #3330: AQS, 1992, 152 pages, softbound, $18.95
- **Nancy Crow: Quilts and Influences,** Nancy Crow, #1981: AQS, 1990, 256 pages, 9 x 12, hardcover, $29.95
- **Nancy Crow: Work in Transition,** Nancy Crow, #3331: AQS, 1992, 32 pages, 9 x 10, softbound, $12.95
- **New Jersey Quilts – 1777 to 1950: Contributions to an American Tradition,** The Heritage Quilt Project of New Jersey; text by Rachel Cochran, Rita Erickson, Natalie Hart & Barbara Schaffer, #3332: AQS, 1992, 256 pages, softbound, $29.95
- **No Dragons on My Quilt,** Jean Ray Laury with Ritva Laury & Lizabeth Laury, #2153: AQS, 1990, 52 pages, hardcover, $12.95
- **Oklahoma Heritage Quilts,** Oklahoma Quilt Heritage Project #2032: AQS, 1990, 144 pages, softbound, $19.95
- **Old Favorites in Miniature,** Tina Gravatt #3469: AQS, 1993, 104 pages, softbound, $15.95
- **A Patchwork of Pieces,** compiled by Cuesta Ray Benberry and Carol Pinney Crabb, #3333: AQS, 1993, 360 pages, softbound, $14.95
- **Quilt Groups Today: Who They Are, Where They Meet, What They Do, and How to Contact Them; A Complete Guide for 1992-1993,** #3308: AQS, 1992, 336 pages, softbound, $14.95
- **Quilter's Registry,** Lynne Fritz, #2380: AQS, 1992, 80 pages, hardbound, $9.95
- **Quilting Patterns from Native American Designs,** Dr. Joyce Mori, #3467: AQS, 1993, 80 pages, softbound, $12.95
- **Quilting with Style: Principles for Great Pattern Design,** Gwen Marston & Joe Cunningham #3470: AQS, 1993, 192 pages, 9 x 12, hardbound, $24.95
- **Quiltmaker's Guide: Basics & Beyond,** Carol Doak, #2284: AQS, 1992, 208 pages, softbound, $19.95
- **Quilts: Old & New, A Similar View,** Paul D. Pilgrim and Gerald E. Roy, #3715: AQS, 1993, 40 pages, softbound, $12.95
- **Quilts: The Permanent Collection – MAQS,** #2257: AQS, 1991, 100 pages, 10 x 6½, softbound, $9.95
- **Seasons of the Heart & Home: Quilts for a Winter's Day,** Jan Patek, #3796: AQS, 1993, 160 pages, softbound, $18.95
- **Seasons of the Heart & Home: Quilts for Summer Days,** Jan Patek, #3761: AQS, 1993, 160 pages, softbound, $18.95
- **Sensational Scrap Quilts,** Darra Duffy Williamson, #2357: AQS, 1992, 152 pages, softbound, $24.95
- **Sets & Borders,** Gwen Marston & Joe Cunningham, #1821: AQS, 1987, 104 pages, softbound, $14.95
- **Show Me Helen...How to Use Quilting Designs,** Helen Squire, #3375: AQS, 1993, 155 pages, softbound, $15.95
- **Somewhere in Between: Quilts and Quilters of Illinois,** Rita Barrow Barber, #1790: AQS, 1986, 78 pages, softbound, $14.95
- **Spike & Zola: Patterns Designed for Laughter...and Appliqué, Painting, & Stenciling,** Donna French Collins, #3794: AQS, 1993, 72 pages, softbound, $9.95
- **Stenciled Quilts for Christmas,** Marie Monteith Sturmer, #2098: AQS, 1990, 104 pages, softbound, $14.95
- **A Treasury of Quilting Designs,** Linda Goodmon Emery, #2029: AQS, 1990, 80 pages, 14 x 11, spiral-bound, $14.95
- **Wonderful Wearables: A Celebration of Creative Clothing,** Virginia Avery, #2286: AQS, 1991, 184 pages, softbound, $24.95

These books can be found in local bookstores and quilt shops. If you are unable to locate a title in your area, you can order by mail from AQS, P.O. Box 3290, Paducah, KY 42002-3290.
Please add $1 for the first book and 40¢ for each additional one to cover postage and handling.
(International orders please add $1.50 for the first book and $1 for each additional one.)